NATIONAL GEOGRAPHIC

Our World

This atlas belongs to

_____

Our World

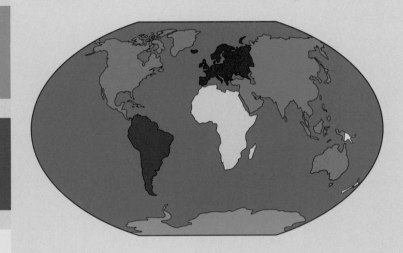

Earth to Globe **4**

Earth as a Map **6**

Looking at the Land **8**

Land and Water **10**

Where People Live **12**

Editor's Note: This atlas will introduce very young children to the most basic concepts of geography: the seven continents, the four oceans that border them, and the countries located on them. With the help of our world-famous cartographers, the simplified maps have been designed to resemble giant puzzle pieces—boldly colored and easy to read. Children will be able to find most of the world's countries on them. Only the very smallest countries have been omitted to keep the maps uncluttered and readable.

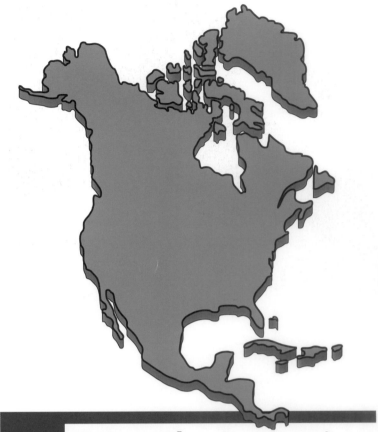

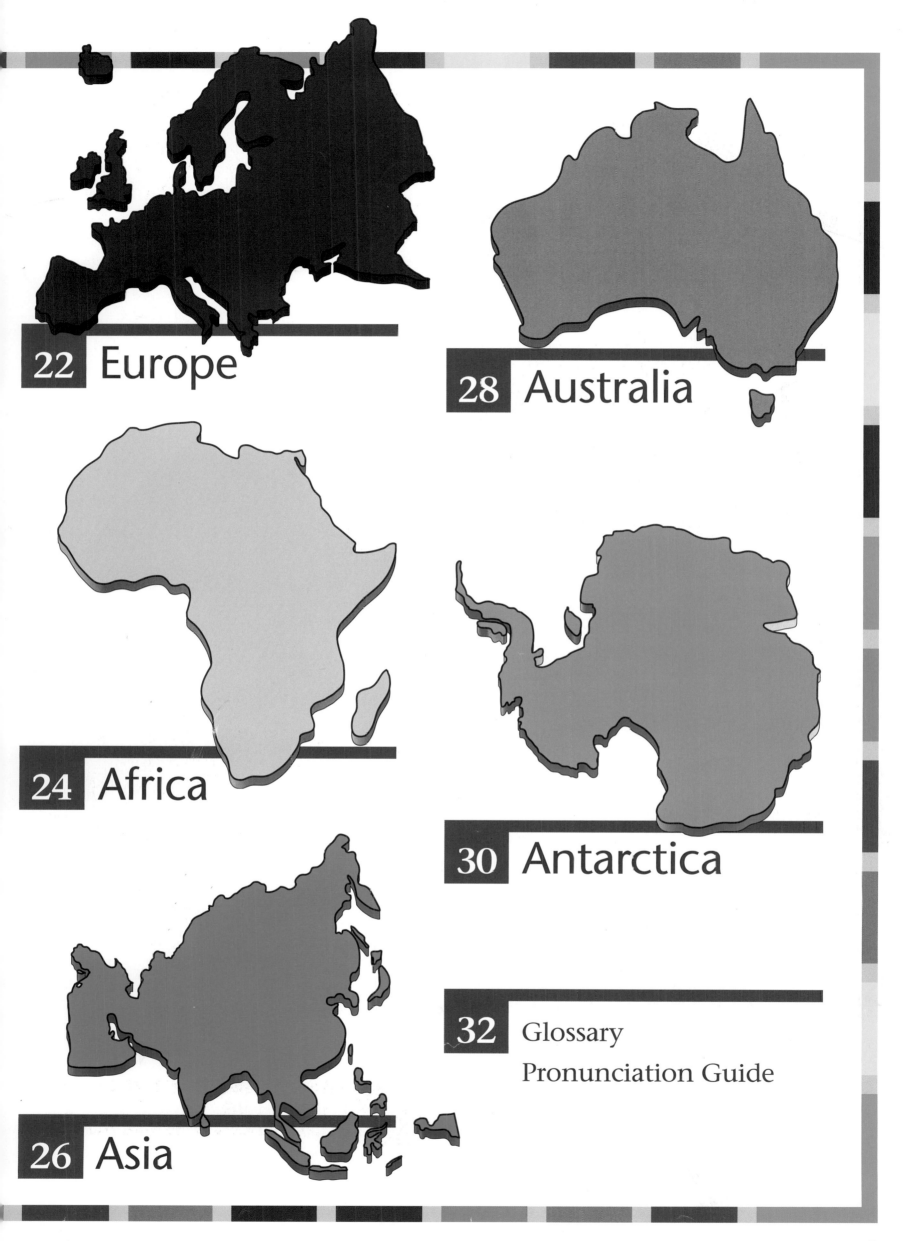

3

Earth to Globe

When astronauts take a rocket ship into space, they see that planet Earth is really an enormous round ball. A globe is a small, round model of Earth. On a globe you see the planet as the astronauts do—one side at a time.

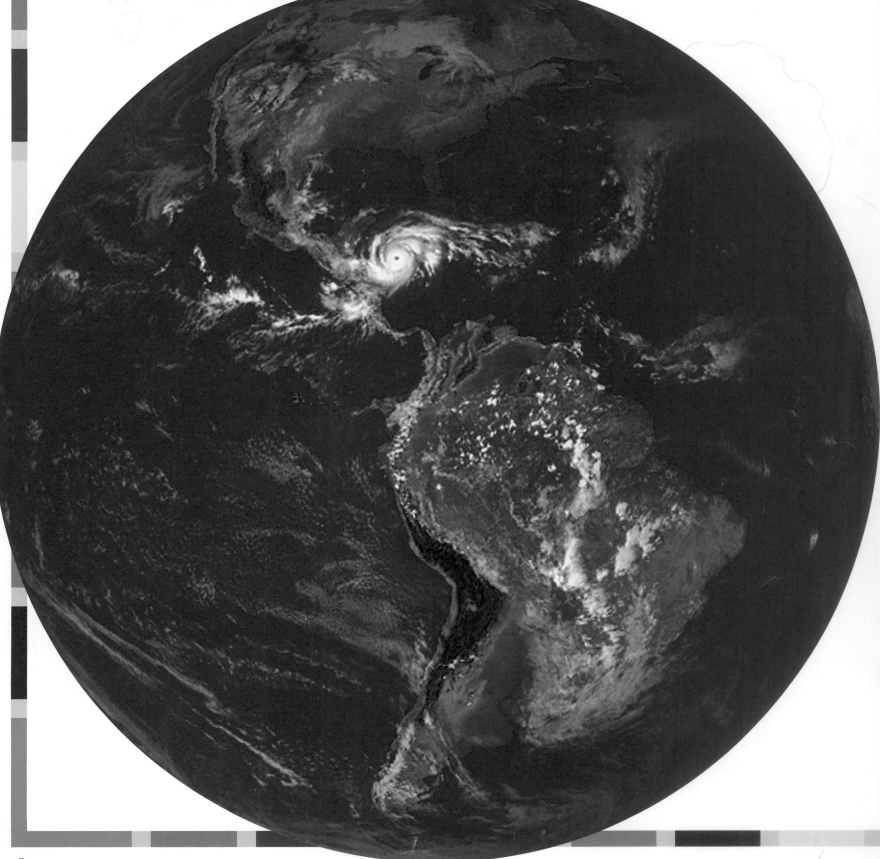

To see what's on the other side of a **globe,** all you have to do is turn it.

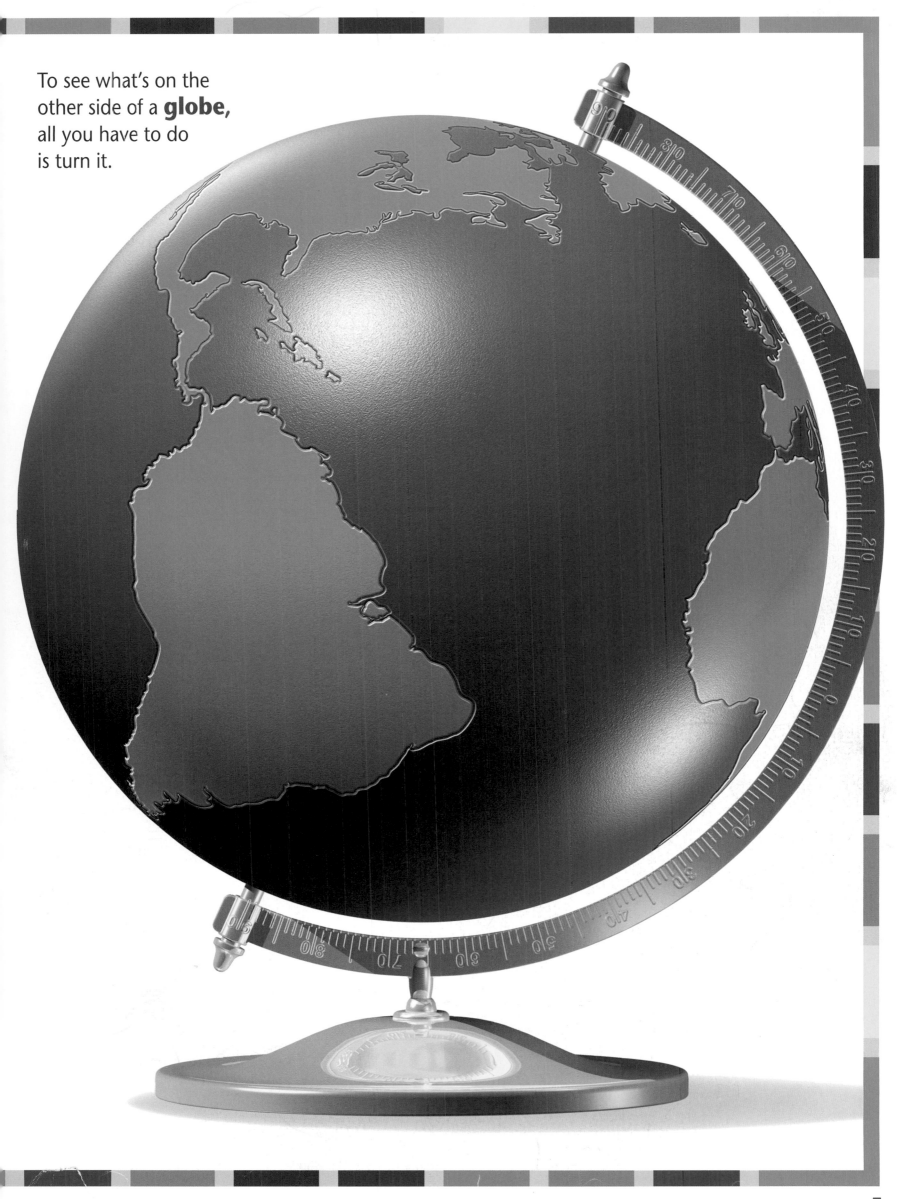

Earth as a Map

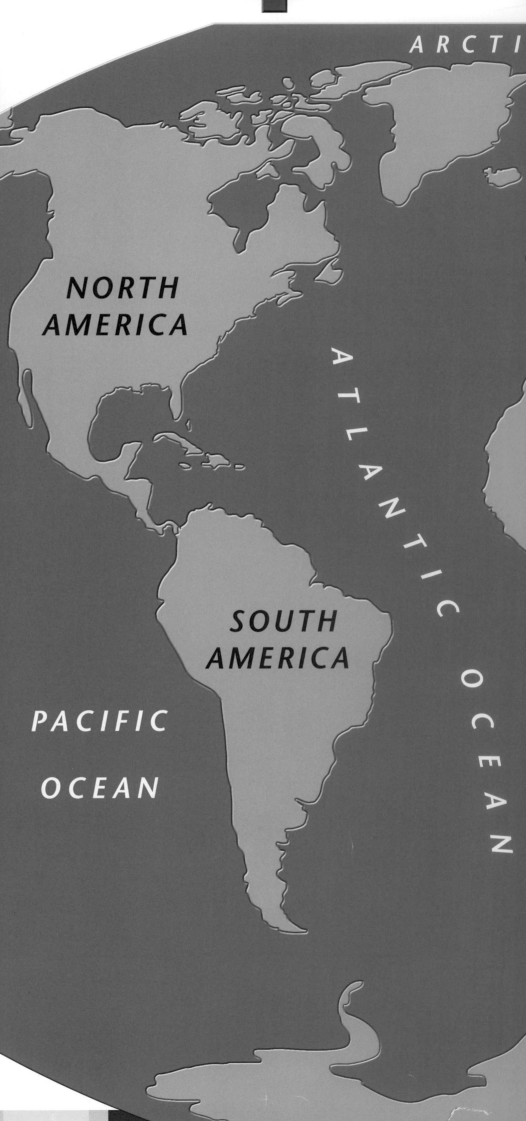

A map is a flat drawing of Earth. It lets you see the whole Earth at one time. This map shows water in blue and land in green. The biggest pieces of land are called continents. The largest bodies of water are called oceans.

A compass like the one below shows directions on a map. For all the maps in this atlas, north (N) is at the top of the page, south (S) is at the bottom, east (E) is at the right edge of the page, and west (W) is at the left edge.

ARCTI

NORTH AMERICA

ATLANTIC OCEAN

SOUTH AMERICA

PACIFIC OCEAN

W

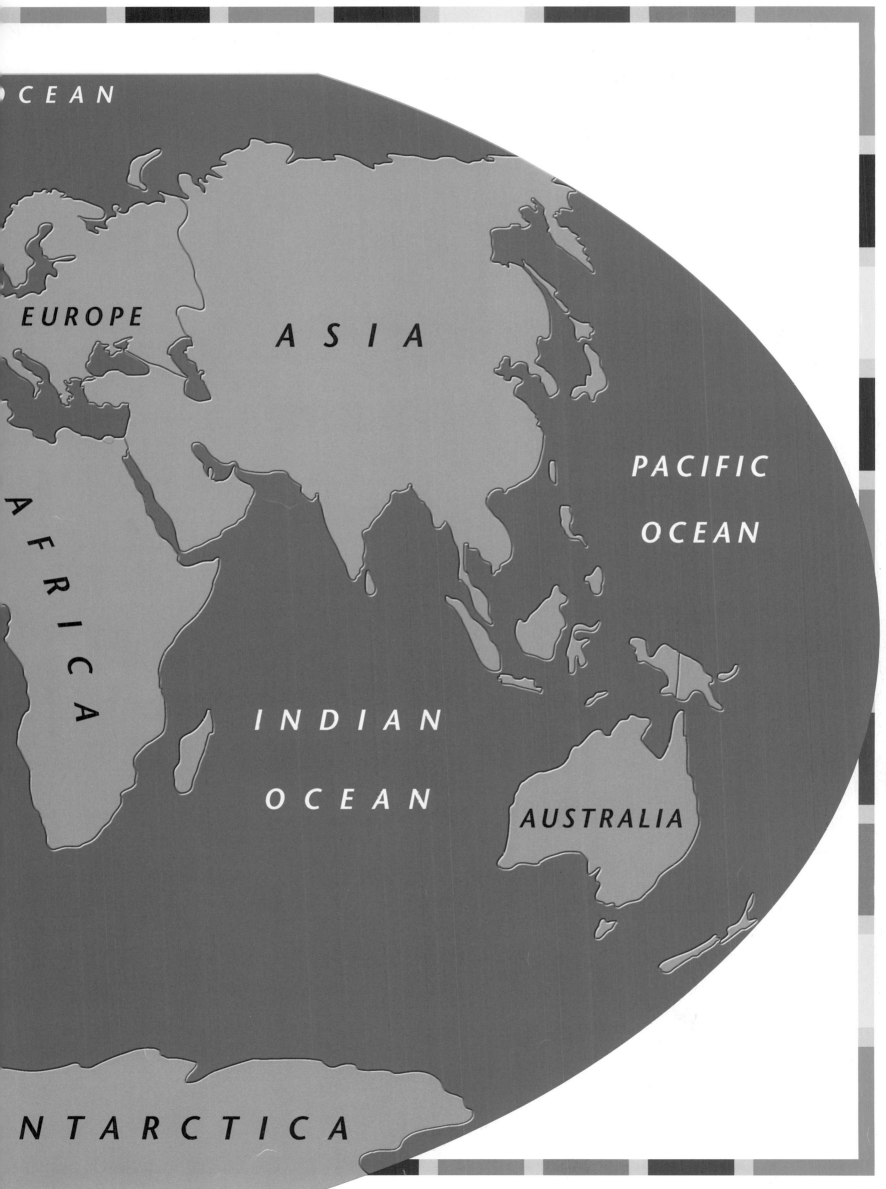

OCEAN

EUROPE

ASIA

AFRICA

PACIFIC

OCEAN

INDIAN

OCEAN

AUSTRALIA

NTARCTICA

E

Looking at the Land

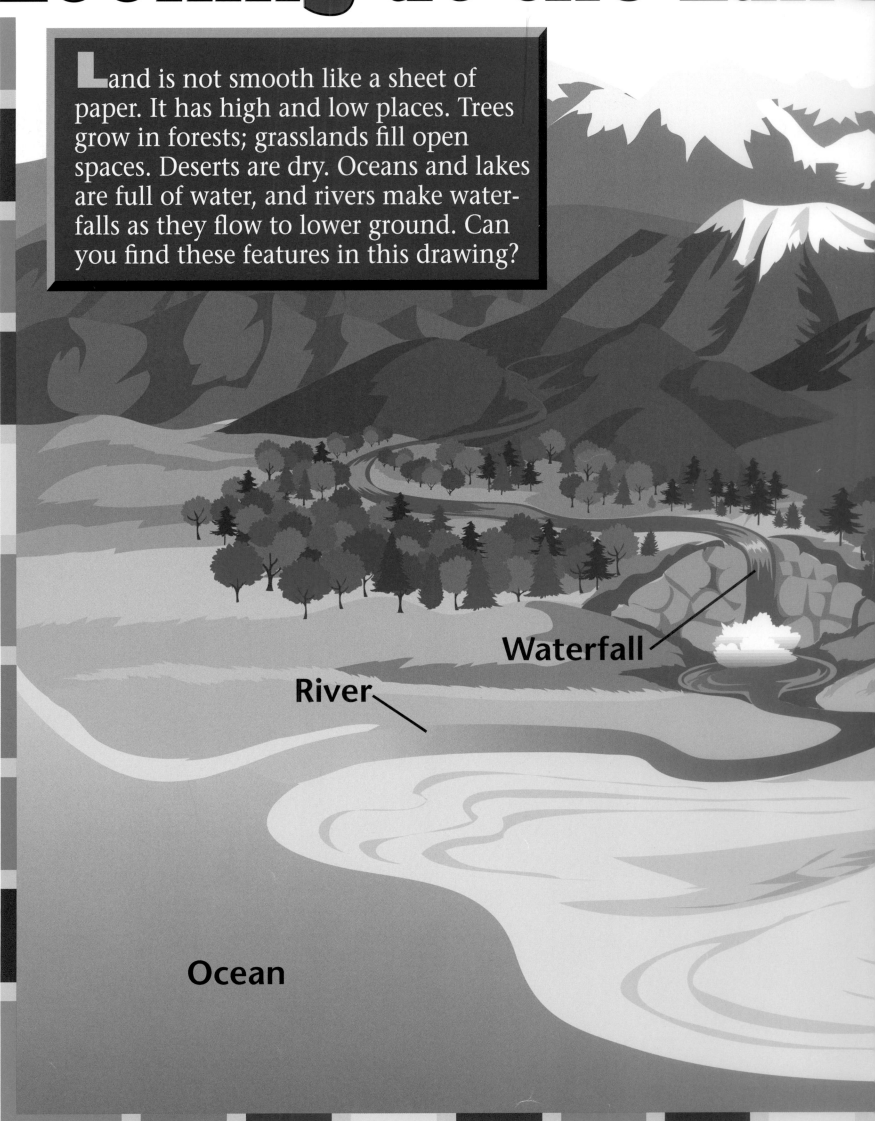

Land is not smooth like a sheet of paper. It has high and low places. Trees grow in forests; grasslands fill open spaces. Deserts are dry. Oceans and lakes are full of water, and rivers make waterfalls as they flow to lower ground. Can you find these features in this drawing?

Waterfall

River

Ocean

Mountains

Volcano

Lake

Forest

Grassland

Desert

Land and Water

Maps can use tiny drawings to show what Earth's surface looks like. A map can't show everything. The key below tells you what things are shown on this one. This map names some of Earth's most important features.

ARCTIC

GREENLAND

ROCKY MOUNTAINS

NORTH AMERICA

Mississippi River

APPALACHIAN MTS.

WEST INDIES

ATLANTIC OCEAN

PACIFIC OCEAN

ANDES

Amazon River

SOUTH AMERICA

ANDES

Map Key

 Mountain

 Desert

 Forest

 Grassland

 Wetland

 Tundra

 Ice Cap

W

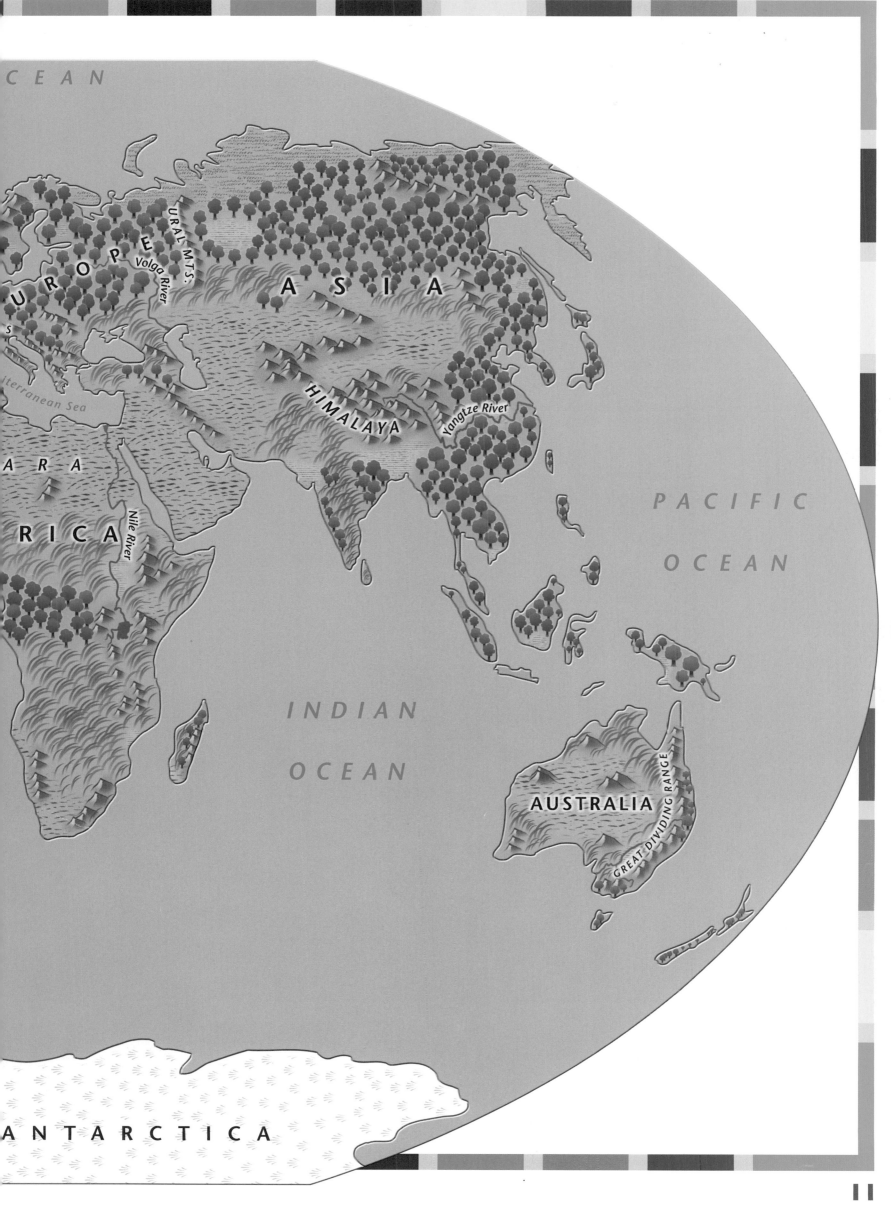

CEAN

EUROPE

URAL MTS.

Volga River

S

Mediterranean Sea

A S I A

ARA

RICA

Nile River

HIMALAYA

Yangtze River

PACIFIC

OCEAN

INDIAN

OCEAN

AUSTRALIA

GREAT DIVIDING RANGE

E

ANTARCTICA

Where People Live

People live in many countries around the world. This map shows countries in different colors so it's easy to see where one country ends and another begins. This map names many but not all of the countries in the world.

W

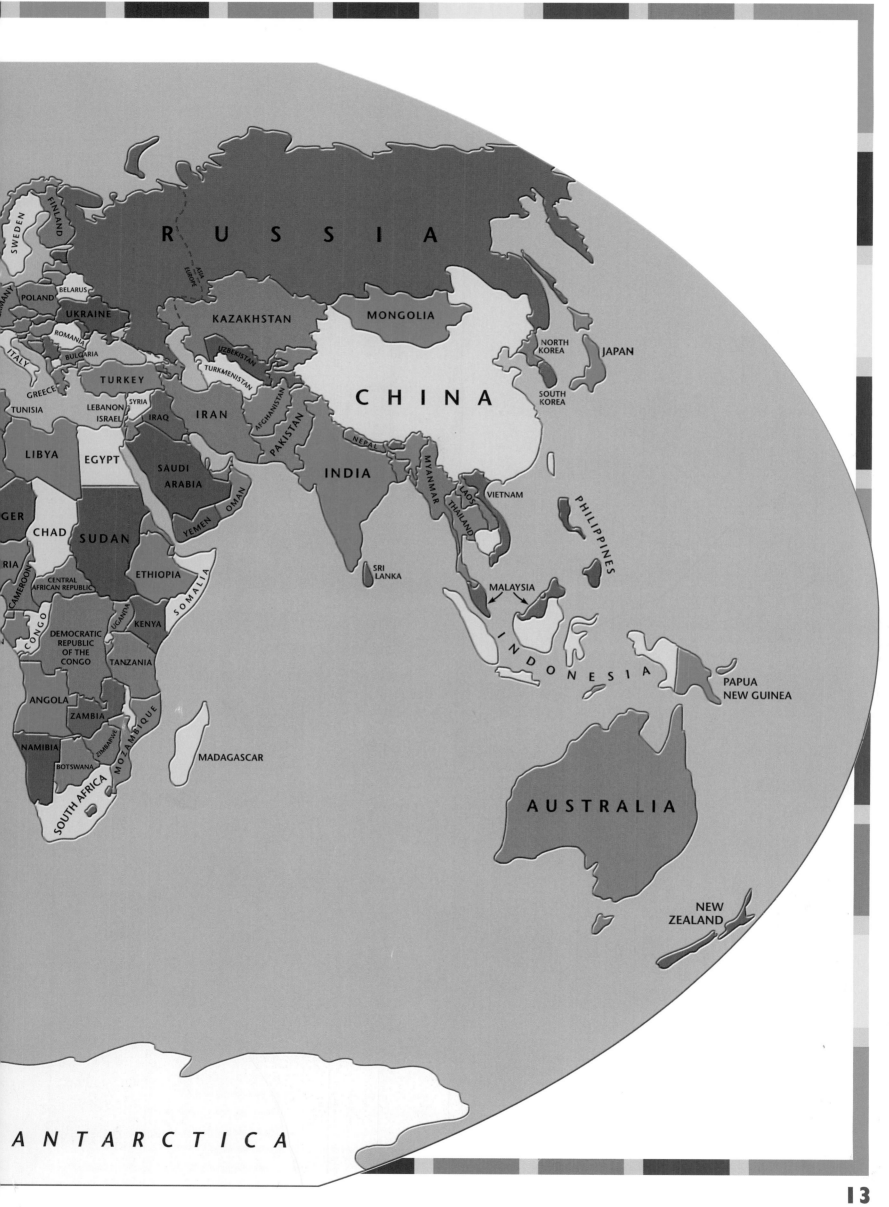

SWEDEN
FINLAND
POLAND
BELARUS
UKRAINE
ROMANIA
ITALY
BULGARIA
GREECE
TURKEY
TUNISIA
LEBANON
SYRIA
ISRAEL
IRAQ
IRAN
LIBYA
EGYPT
SAUDI
ARABIA
GER
CHAD
SUDAN
RIA
YEMEN
OMAN
CAMEROON
CENTRAL
AFRICAN REPUBLIC
ETHIOPIA
SOMALIA
CONGO
UGANDA
DEMOCRATIC
REPUBLIC
OF THE
CONGO
KENYA
TANZANIA
ANGOLA
ZAMBIA
ZIMBABWE
NAMIBIA
MOZAMBIQUE
BOTSWANA
SOUTH AFRICA
MADAGASCAR

RUSSIA
ASIA
EUROPE
KAZAKHSTAN
MONGOLIA
NORTH
KOREA
JAPAN
UZBEKISTAN
TURKMENISTAN
CHINA
SOUTH
KOREA
AFGHANISTAN
PAKISTAN
NEPAL
INDIA
MYANMAR
LAOS
VIETNAM
THAILAND
PHILIPPINES
SRI
LANKA
MALAYSIA
INDONESIA
PAPUA
NEW GUINEA

AUSTRALIA

NEW
ZEALAND

ANTARCTICA

North America

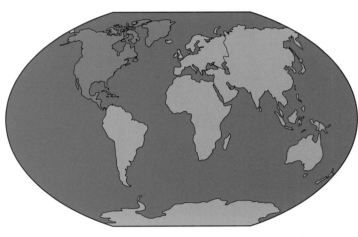

School is out! We live on one of the islands in the West Indies. These islands are part of North America. Greenland is, too. Our continent stretches from Canada all the way to Panama. Most people in North America speak English, Spanish, or French.

◄**Polar bears** live in the far north where there is ice and snow year-round. White fur helps them hide against the snow.

▼In North America farmers grow wheat, corn, and other crops. These farmers are **harvesting wheat** in Canada.

Find These On the Map

Mount McKinley is North America's highest mountain. It is also called Denali. Look for it in the northernmost U.S. state.

The Panama Canal is a waterway across Panama. Ships use it as a shortcut between the Atlantic and the Pacific Ocean.

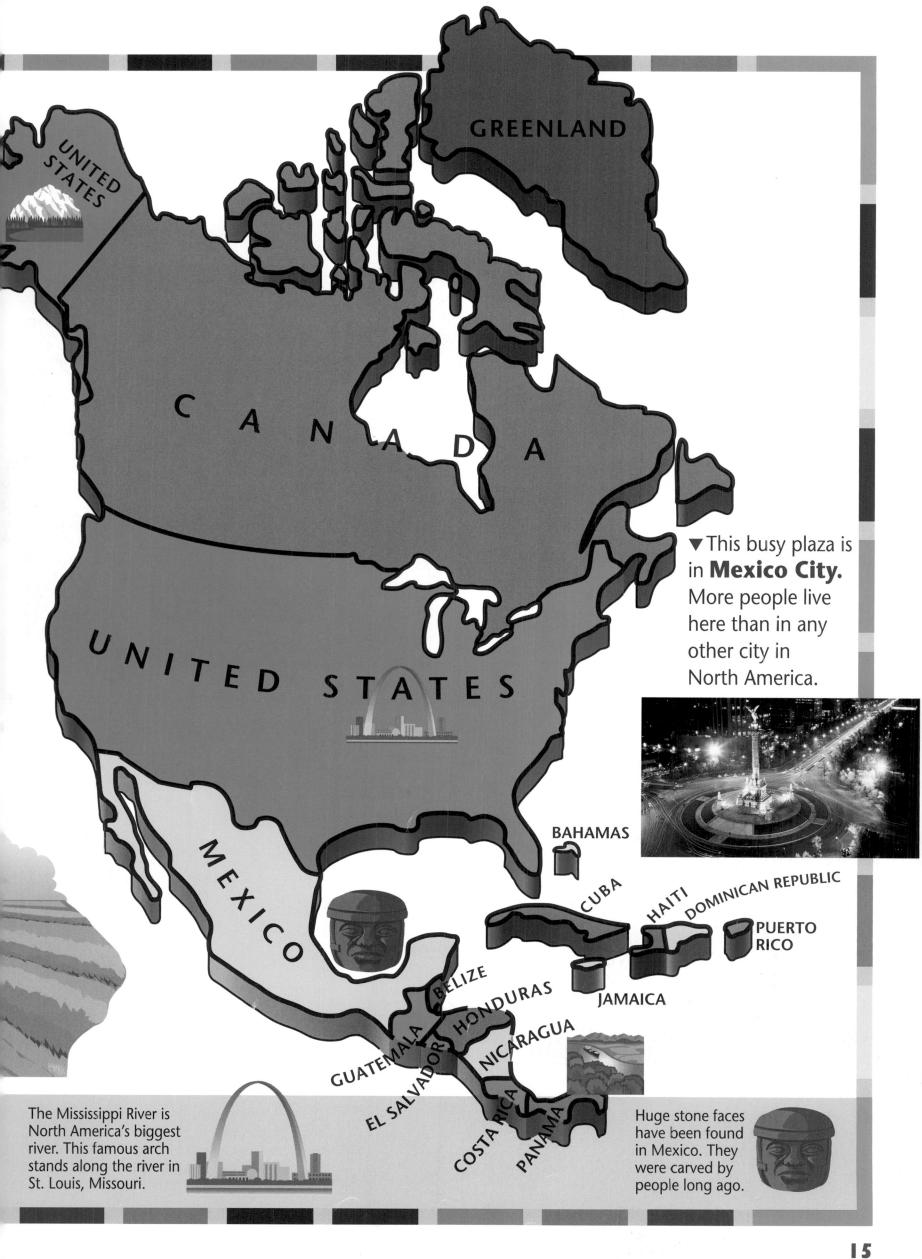

GREENLAND

UNITED STATES

C A N A D A

UNITED STATES

▼ This busy plaza is in **Mexico City.** More people live here than in any other city in North America.

BAHAMAS

M E X I C O

CUBA

HAITI

DOMINICAN REPUBLIC

PUERTO RICO

JAMAICA

BELIZE

HONDURAS

GUATEMALA

EL SALVADOR

NICARAGUA

COSTA RICA

PANAMA

The Mississippi River is North America's biggest river. This famous arch stands along the river in St. Louis, Missouri.

Huge stone faces have been found in Mexico. They were carved by people long ago.

15

United States

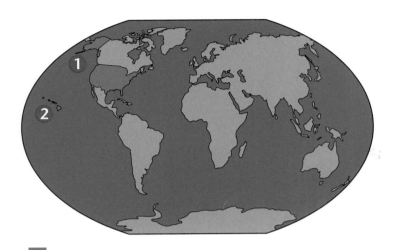

It's pumpkin-carving time! In the United States we hollow out pumpkins to make jack o' lanterns in autumn. The United States is on the continent of North America. People from all over the world live here. We call ourselves Americans.

◄ The **space shuttle** is a special rocket ship. The United States uses the shuttle to carry astronauts, scientists, and equipment into space and back.

ALASKA

❶

Map note: To see the real locations of the states of Alaska and Hawai'i, look at the small world map (top left).

Find These On the Map

There are many volcanoes in Hawai'i and Alaska. Washington, Oregon, and California have some, too.

The Everglades is a huge swampy place in Florida. Alligators, birds, and lots of other animals live there.

▶ **Tornadoes** are powerful, funnel-shaped winds. They sometimes come with thunderstorms. The United States has more tornadoes than any other country in the world.

MONTANA

NORTH DAKOTA

MINNESOTA

MICHIGAN

WISCONSIN

NEW HAMPSHIRE

VERMONT

MAINE

AHO

SOUTH DAKOTA

NEW YORK

MASSACHUSETTS

WYOMING

IOWA

PENNSYLVANIA

RHODE ISLAND

CONNECTICUT

NEBRASKA

ILLINOIS

INDIANA

OHIO

NEW JERSEY

UTAH

DELAWARE

COLORADO

KANSAS

MISSOURI

WEST VIRGINIA

VIRGINIA

MARYLAND

KENTUCKY

ZONA

NEW MEXICO

OKLAHOMA

ARKANSAS

TENNESSEE

NORTH CAROLINA

SOUTH CAROLINA

TEXAS

MISSISSIPPI

ALABAMA

GEORGIA

LOUISIANA

FLORIDA

❷

HAWAI'I
ain Islands)

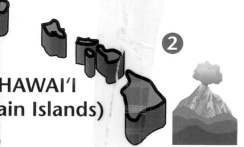

▶ The **Statue of Liberty** stands at the entrance to New York harbor. This symbol of freedom welcomes people to the United States.

The President of the United States lives in the White House. It is in Washington, D.C., the capital city.

Old Faithful is a spout of hot water. It shoots out of the ground in Yellowstone National Park.

Canada

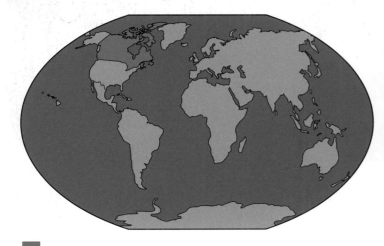

Let's go out and play! We live in the Yukon Territory. There are lots of wide-open spaces here. Mostly native people called Inuit live in northern Canada. All the big cities are much farther south. The chief languages are English and French.

YUKON TERRITORY

BRITISH COLUMBIA

▶ The **Winterlude Festival** is held in Ottawa, Canada's capital city. It celebrates winter with snow sculptures, the worlds longest ice-skating rink, and a playground made of snow!

Find These On the Map

Native people in British Columbia carve colorful totem poles to honor their history and the spirits of their ancestors.

Cowboys ride broncos and bulls at the Calgary Stampede. This rodeo takes place each summer in Alberta.

▲ Olympic Stadium, with its huge tower, was built for the winter Olympic Games. It is in Montreal, the largest city in Quebec.

NUNAVUT

NORTHWEST TERRITORIES

ALBERTA

SASKATCHEWAN

MANITOBA

ONTARIO

QUEBEC

NEWFOUNDLAND AND LABRADOR

NEW BRUNSWICK

NOVA SCOTIA

PRINCE EDWARD ISLAND

◀ The Rocky Mountains in western Canada are a popular vacation spot. People come to canoe, hike, ski, and rock climb.

Caribou live in Canada's far north. In the summer they eat a lot of food so they won't be hungry during the long winter.

The Canadian National Tower is the world's tallest tower and one of Canada's most famous places. It is in Toronto, Ontario, Canada's biggest city.

South America

Fish for dinner, anyone? We caught this big fish in the Amazon River. I live in Brazil. It is the biggest country in South America. People in Brazil speak Portuguese. In almost every other country in South America people speak Spanish.

▼ Cowboys called **gauchos** herd cattle in grassy parts of Argentina and Uruguay. Beef is a popular food in South America.

Find These On the Map

Angel Falls is the highest waterfall in the world. To find it, you'd have to hike through the rain forest in Venezuela.

The Andes are high, snow-covered mountains. They stretch along the west coast from Colombia all the way to the tip of Chile.

VENEZUELA

COLOMBIA

ECUADOR

GUYANA

SURINAME

FRENCH GUIANA

P E R U

B R A Z I L

BOLIVIA

PARAGUAY

C H I L E

A R G E N T I N A

URUGUAY

▶ Farmers in Ecuador ship **bananas** to markets all over the world.

▼ Macaws are big, colorful birds. They live in the **rain forest** that grows along the Amazon River. Jaguars and monkeys live there, too.

▲ Every year people celebrate **carnival** in Brazil. They dress up in colorful costumes and parade through the streets.

Llamas are good at climbing mountains. People in the Andes use them to carry things. They also make warm blankets and ponchos from llama wool.

Some houses along the Amazon River stand on stilts. This huge river flows from Peru across Brazil to the Atlantic Ocean.

Europe

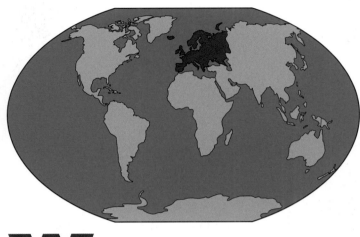

Would anyone like a pony ride? We live in Ireland, an island country in Europe. Europe has many long fingers of land called peninsulas that stick out into the sea. This means no place is very far from the water.

◄**Big Ben** is the bell in a famous clock tower in London. London is the capital city of the United Kingdom.

Find These On the Map

St. Basil's is the most famous church in Russia. The colorful rooftops are called onion domes because of their shape.

Iceland has more than 100 volcanoes and many hot springs. This island country also has many huge rivers of ice called glaciers.

Map note: The broken lines on the map mean the rest of these countries are in Asia. Look at the map on pages 26–27.

NORWAY

SWEDEN

FINLAND

RUSSIA

EUROPE

ASIA

UNITED KINGDOM

DENMARK

ESTONIA

LATVIA

LITHUANIA

RUSSIA

BELARUS

KAZAKHSTAN

NETHER-LANDS

BELGIUM

GERMANY

POLAND

EMBOURG

CZECH REPUBLIC

SLOVAKIA

UKRAINE

SWITZERLAND

AUSTRIA

HUNGARY

MOLDOVA

SLOVENIA

CROATIA

ROMANIA

AZERBAIJAN

GEORGIA

ITALY

FRANCE

BOSNIA & HERZEGOVINA

SERBIA & MONTENEGRO

BULGARIA

ITALY

MACEDONIA

TURKEY

ITALY

ALBANIA

GREECE

CYPRUS

◀This woman is picking **grapes.** They are one of the many kinds of fruit that grow in southern Europe. Here, the weather is warm and sunny.

▲ Venice is a city in Italy. People there often travel along the city's canals in boats called **gondolas.**

Long ago, people in Greece believed gods and goddesses ruled Earth. This god lived in a castle beneath the sea.

The Eiffel Tower is a famous structure in Paris, France. For many years it was the tallest building in the world.

Africa

WESTERN
SAHARA

MAURIT

SENEGAL

GAMBIA

GUINEA-
BISSAU

GUINEA

SIERRA LEONE

LIBERIA

Maasai girls like to wear colorful bead-work. Our families herd cattle in East Africa. Most people in Africa are farmers or herders. Africa has more countries than any other continent. More than a thousand languages are spoken here.

▼**Savannas** are grasslands that cover large areas in Africa. Herds of antelopes, zebras, elephants, and other animals graze here. Cheetahs come to hunt these animals for food.

▶Only male **lions,** like this one, have a mane of hair around their heads. Lions live on Africa's grasslands in groups called prides.

Find These On the Map

Snow-capped Mount Kilimanjaro, in Tanzania, is the highest mountain in Africa.

In South Africa, miners dig for diamonds, gold, and other valuable materials. Mining is a dangerous job.

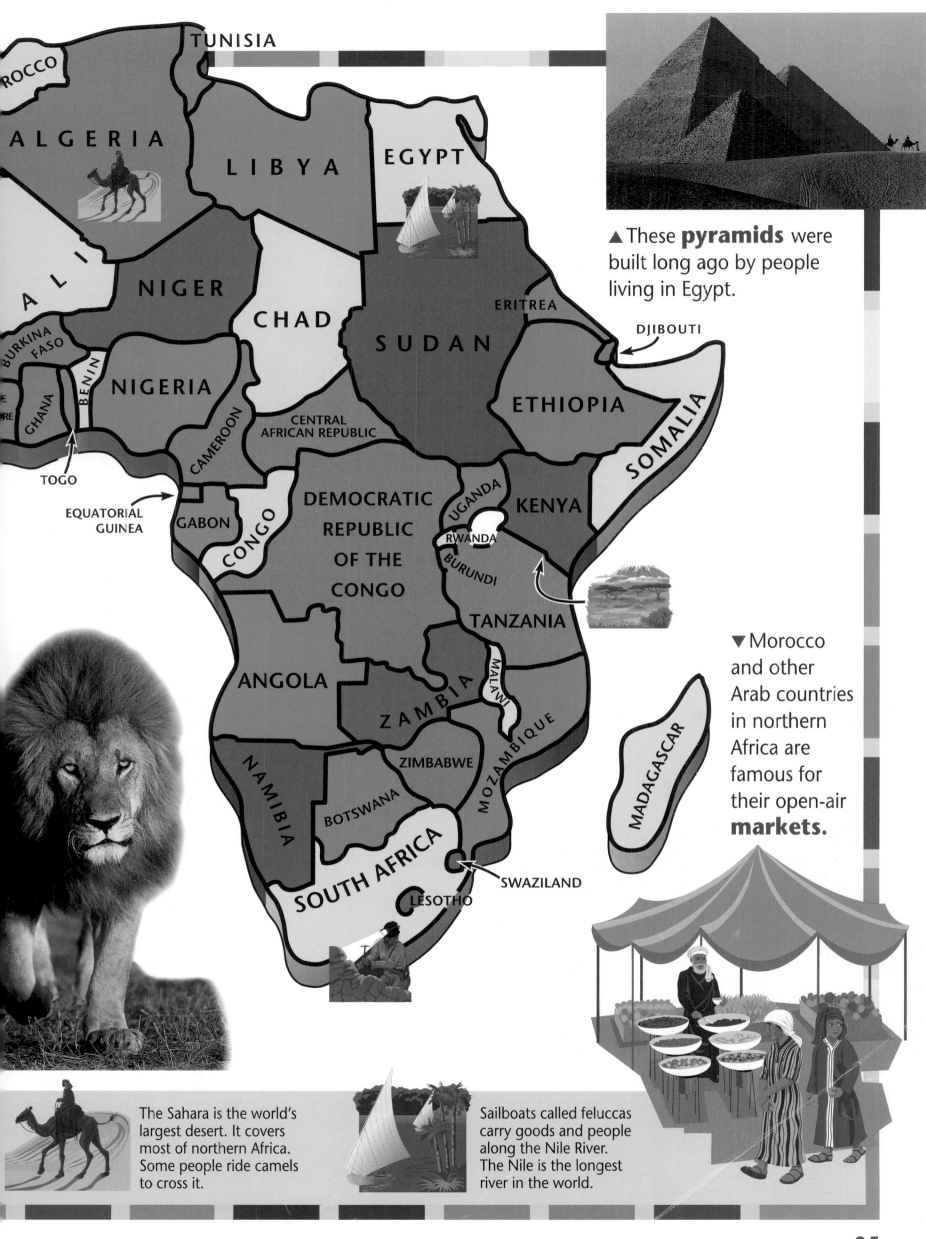

ROCCO

TUNISIA

ALGERIA

LIBYA

EGYPT

▲ These **pyramids** were built long ago by people living in Egypt.

ALI

NIGER

CHAD

SUDAN

ERITREA

DJIBOUTI

BURKINA FASO

BENIN

NIGERIA

CAMEROON

CENTRAL AFRICAN REPUBLIC

ETHIOPIA

SOMALIA

GHANA

TOGO

EQUATORIAL GUINEA

GABON

CONGO

DEMOCRATIC REPUBLIC OF THE CONGO

UGANDA

RWANDA

BURUNDI

KENYA

TANZANIA

▼ Morocco and other Arab countries in northern Africa are famous for their open-air **markets.**

ANGOLA

ZAMBIA

MALAWI

NAMIBIA

ZIMBABWE

MOZAMBIQUE

MADAGASCAR

BOTSWANA

SOUTH AFRICA

SWAZILAND

LESOTHO

The Sahara is the world's largest desert. It covers most of northern Africa. Some people ride camels to cross it.

Sailboats called feluccas carry goods and people along the Nile River. The Nile is the longest river in the world.

Asia

Welcome to Asia! I live in a part of China called Tibet. More people live in China than in any other country in Asia. This continent has the most people, the most land, and the highest mountains on Earth.

◄ Bamboo is the **panda's** favorite food. In the wild these animals live only in China in places where bamboo forests grow.

Find These On the Map

 Mount Everest is the highest mountain in the world. It is almost six miles high!

 The Great Wall of China was built hundreds of years ago to keep out enemies. It is about 3,000 miles long.

Map note: The broken lines on the map mean that the rest of these countries are in Europe. Look at the map on pages 22–23.

EUROPE

ASIA

AIJAN

KAZAKHSTAN

UZBEKISTAN

ENISTAN

KYRGYZSTAN

TAJIKISTAN

AFGHANISTAN

PAKISTAN

R U S S I A

MONGOLIA

NEPAL

BHUTAN

C H I N A

INDIA

MYANMAR (BURMA)

LAOS

THAILAND

BANGLADESH

CAMBODIA

VIETNAM

SRI LANKA

NORTH KOREA

SOUTH KOREA

JAPAN

PHILIPPINES

BRUNEI

M A L A Y S I A

I N D O N E S I A

TIMOR-LESTE (EAST TIMOR)

▼Many people in India believe the **Ganges River** has the power to heal the sick. Millions of people live along its banks and bathe in it.

◄Rice is the main food eaten in Asia. Farmers often grow it on steplike fields called **terraces.** These fields are cut into steep hillsides.

The city of Jerusalem is a religious center for Jews, Christians, and Muslims. Most of the world's major religions began in Asia.

Japan is a very high-tech country. Its fastest trains are called bullet trains. They carry millions of people to and from work each day.

Australia

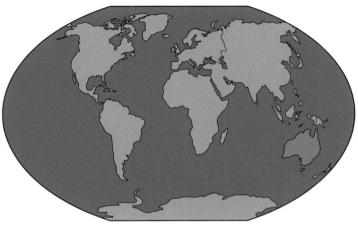

▲ Australia has lots of **sheep.** Here, a rancher herds sheep into a pen.

ook, I've found a starfish! Australia's Great Barrier Reef is full of all kinds of sea life. Water is all around Australia, but there is very little water on the land. Australia is the smallest continent. It is also the only one that has just one country—Australia!

▼ Many roads in Australia are straight and flat. That's because most of Australia is **desert.** Drivers here have to be on the look out for kangaroos!

Find These On the Map

The roof of the Sydney Opera House looks like sails on a boat. Sydney is Australia's largest city.

The Tasmanian devil raises its young in a pouch on its belly. It is called "devil" because it makes screamlike noises.

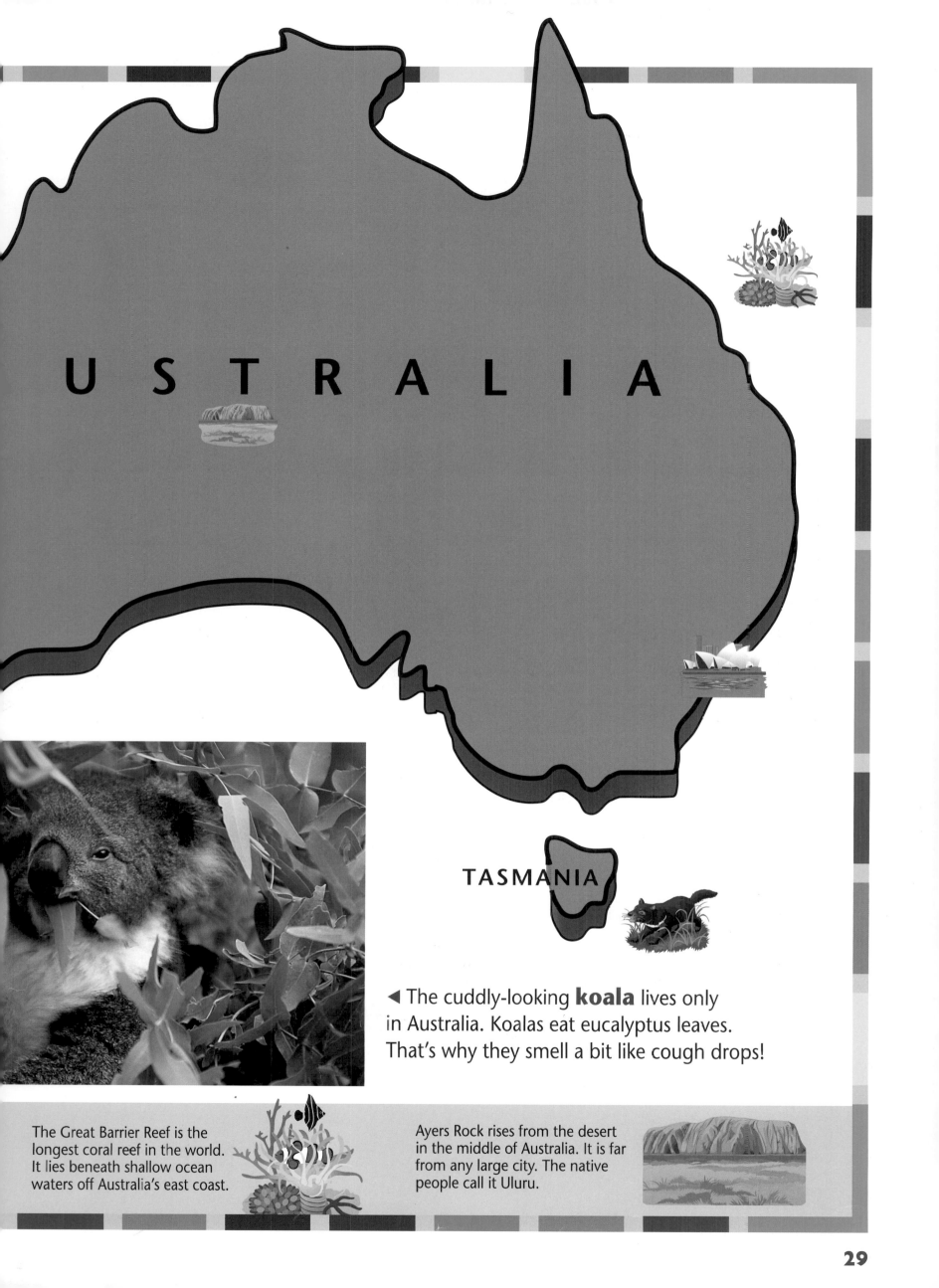

USTRALIA

TASMANIA

◄ The cuddly-looking **koala** lives only in Australia. Koalas eat eucalyptus leaves. That's why they smell a bit like cough drops!

The Great Barrier Reef is the longest coral reef in the world. It lies beneath shallow ocean waters off Australia's east coast.

Ayers Rock rises from the desert in the middle of Australia. It is far from any large city. The native people call it Uluru.

Antarctica

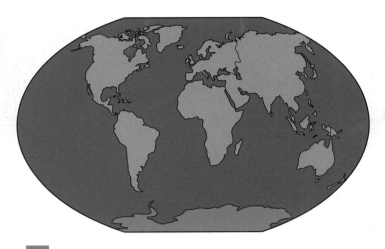

If you visited Antarctica, you would see penguins and seals, mountains and valleys, and snow and ice. The continent is so cold, people come only for visits, not to live. There aren't any cities, but you will find scientists at work. Antarctica is the only continent that has no countries.

◄ **Scientists** come to Antarctica from other continents. They stay for a few chilly weeks or months. These researchers are using a balloon to study the weather.

Find These On the Map

Antarctica has many mountains and even some volcanoes. Mount Erebus is the world's southernmost volcano.

The South Pole is the southernmost point on the Earth. It is marked by flags and a pole.

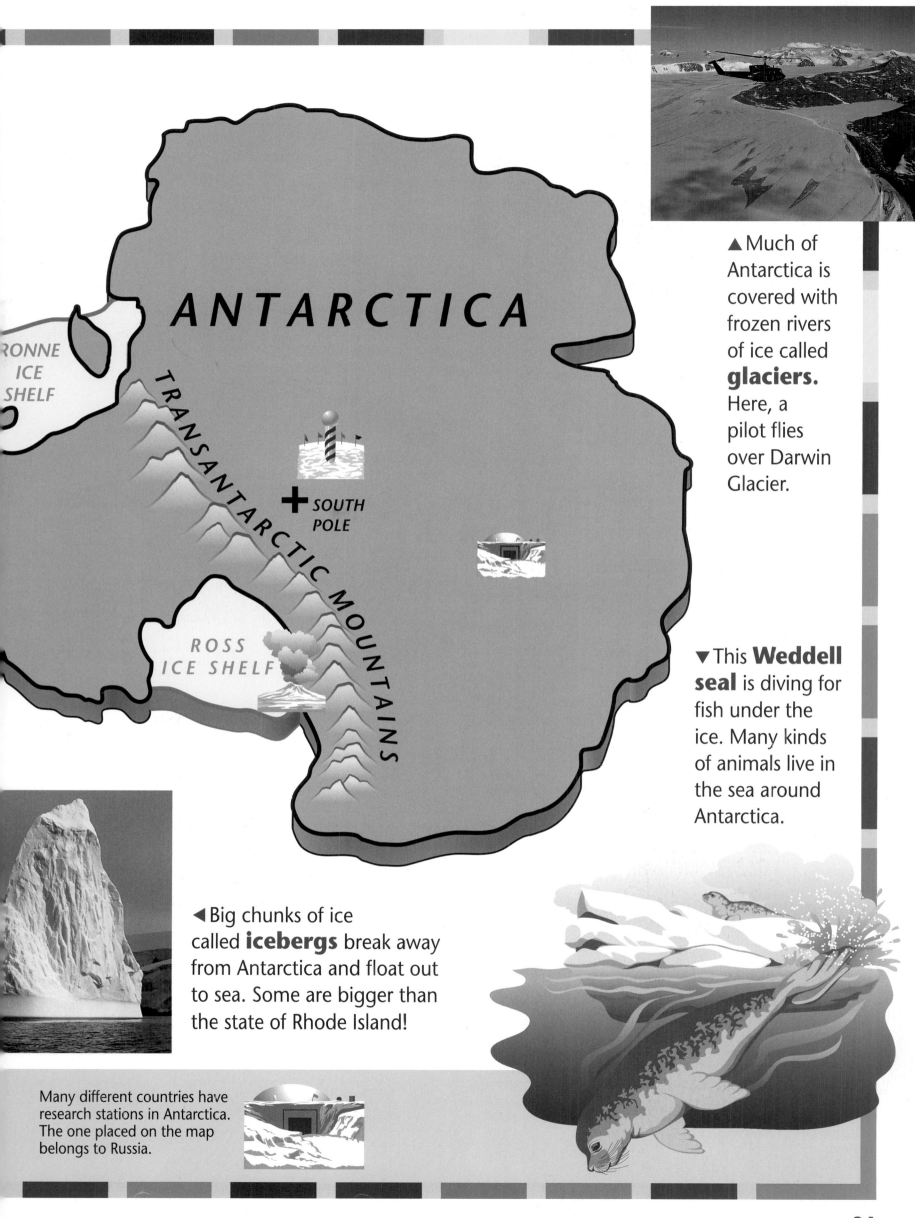

ANTARCTICA

RONNE
ICE
SHELF

TRANSANTARCTIC MOUNTAINS

+ SOUTH
POLE

ROSS
ICE SHELF

▲ Much of Antarctica is covered with frozen rivers of ice called **glaciers.** Here, a pilot flies over Darwin Glacier.

▼ This **Weddell seal** is diving for fish under the ice. Many kinds of animals live in the sea around Antarctica.

◄ Big chunks of ice called **icebergs** break away from Antarctica and float out to sea. Some are bigger than the state of Rhode Island!

Many different countries have research stations in Antarctica. The one placed on the map belongs to Russia.

31

Glossary

canal A canal is a narrow waterway that people have built across the land. The Panama Canal was built across the country of Panama.

capital city A capital city is the place where a country's government is located. Washington, D.C., is the capital city of the United States.

coast A coast is land that borders an ocean.

desert A desert is a place that gets very little rain or snow. It can be sandy or rocky, hot or cold. The Sahara is the world's largest desert.

ice cap An ice cap is a permanent sheet of thick ice that covers land. Greenland and Antarctica both have ice caps.

ice shelf An ice shelf is a thick sheet of ice that sticks out beyond the land into the sea. The largest ice shelves are in Antarctica.

lake A lake is a body of water that is surrounded by land.

mountain A mountain is the highest kind of land. Mount Everest is the highest mountain.

peninsula A peninsula is a piece of land that sticks out into the water. Italy and Florida are examples of peninsulas.

rain forest A rain forest is a woodland that grows in a place that is very wet and usually quite warm. The Amazon rain forest is the largest in the world.

river A river is a large stream of water that flows across the land. The Nile is the world's longest river.

tundra Tundra is a cold region with low plants that grow only during warm months.

volcano A volcano is an opening in the Earth through which melted rock from deep inside the Earth forces its way out onto the surface. Some mountains are volcanoes.

West Indies West Indies is the name for thousands of warm, sunny islands located in the ocean between North America and South America. Cuba is the largest one of these islands.

wetland A wetland is an area of land, such as a swamp or a marsh, that is mostly covered with water. The Everglades is a wetland.

Pronunciation Guide

Note: The accented syllable is in capital letters.

Ayers	ARZ	gondolas	GAHN duh luz
carnival	kar nih VAL	Himalaya	hih MAHL yuh
Denali	duh NAH lee	Kilimanjaro	kih lih mun JAR o
Erebus	ER uh bus	Maasai	MAH sigh
eucalyptus	you kuh LIP tus	Tasmanian	taz MAY nee un
feluccas	fuh LOO kuz	Uluru	oo LOO roo
gauchos	GOW choz		
Ganges	GAN jeez		

National Geographic Society

John M. Fahey, Jr.
President and Chief Executive Officer

Gilbert M. Grosvenor
Chairman of the Board

Nina D. Hoffman
Executive Vice President, President of Books and Education Publishing Group

Ericka Markman
Senior *Vice President, President of Children's Books and Education Publishing Group*

Stephen Mico
Senior Vice President and Publisher, Children's Books and Education Publishing Group

Staff for this book

Nancy Laties Feresten
Vice President, Editor-in-Chief of Children's Books

Suzanne Patrick Fonda
Project Editor

Marianne R. Koszorus
Design Director

Bea Jackson
Design Director, Children's Books and Education Publishing

Carl Mehler
Director of Maps

Sharon Davis Thorpe
David M. Seager
Designers

Susan McGrath
Priyanka Lamichhane
Writers

Marilyn Mofford Gibbons
Lori Epstein
Illustrations Editors

Thomas L. Gray
Map Editor

Matt Chwastyk
Michelle H. Picard
Gregory Ugiansky
Map Research and Production

Marcia Pires-Harwood
Text and Illustration Research

Jo Tunstall
Editorial Assistant

Janet Dustin
Jean Cantu
Illustrations Assistants

R. Gary Colbert
Production Director

Lewis R. Bassford
Production Manager

Vincent P. Ryan
Maryclare Tracey
Manufacturing Managers

Consultants

Peggy Steele Clay
Teacher-in-Residence
National Geographic Society

Billie M. Kapp
Social Studies Consultant
Connecticut Geographic Alliance

Illustrations Credits

Map art by Stuart Armstrong; all other art (unless otherwise indicated) by Barbara Leonard Gibson

Front cover globe digitally created by Slim Films; back cover (upper, left), Kenneth Love/National Geographic Society; (bottom, left), Goodshoot; (bottom, right), George F. Mobley/National Geographic Society; page 4, Hal Pierce: NASA Goddard Laboratory for Atmospheres, data from NOAA; 5 (globe), Slim Films; 6, (compass art), Theophilus Britt Griswold; 14 (upper), Trevor Wood/Getty Images; 14 (lower), Flip Nicklin; 15 Randy Faris/CORBIS; 16 (upper), Lori Adamski-Peek/Getty Images; 16 (lower), Jon Schneeberger; 17 (upper), Edi Ann Otto; 17 (lower), Paul Chesley; 18 (upper) Jay Dickman/CORBIS; 18 (lower) Carl Purcell/CORBIS; 19 (upper) Yves Marcoux/CORBIS; 19 (lower) Paul Chesley; 20, Kenneth Love; 21 (upper), John Marshall/Getty Images; 21 (lower), Orion Press/Getty Images; 22 (upper), Sam Abell; 22 (lower), Marilyn Mofford Gibbons; 23, Todd Gipstein; 24, George F. Mobley; 25 (upper), James L. Stanfield; 25 (lower), Daniel J. Cox/Natural Exposures; 26 (upper), D. E. Cox/Getty Images; 26 (lower), Lu Zhi; 27, Marilyn Mofford Gibbons; 28 (upper), Medford Taylor; 28 (lower), Lonnie Duka/Getty Images; 28–29, Medford Taylor; 30–31 (all), George F. Mobley.

Acknowledgments

We are grateful for the assistance of Gertrude Burr, Director of the Bethesda Montessori School, for her guidance in the initial planning of this atlas.

Original edition copyright © 2000 National Geographic Society
ISBN 0-7922-7576-4

Updated edition featuring United States & Canada copyright © 2006 National Geographic Society
ISBN 0-7922-5531-3 (hardcover)
ISBN 0-7922-5532-1 (library)

One of the world's largest nonprofit scientific and educational organizations, the National Geographic Society was founded in 1888 "for the increase and diffusion of geographic knowledge." Fulfilling this mission, the Society educates and inspires millions every day through its magazines, books, television programs, videos, maps and atlases, research grants, the National Geographic Bee, teacher workshops, and innovative classroom materials. The Society is supported through membership dues, charitable gifts, and income from the sale of its educational products. This support is vital to National Geographic's mission to increase global understanding and promote conservation of our planet through exploration, research, and education.

For more information about the National Geographic Society and its educational programs and publications, please call 1-800-NGS-LINE (647-5463) or write to the following address:

National Geographic Society
1145 17th Street N.W.
Washington, D.C. 20036-4688 U.S.A.

Visit the Society's Web site: www.nationalgeographic.com